PRAYERS FOR EVERY MAN

KEL GROSECLOSE

DIMENSIONS
FOR LIVING
NASHVILLE

A Moment with God for Men:
Prayers for Every Man

Copyright © 1998 by Dimensions for Living

All rights reserved. No part of this work may be reproduced or transmitted in any form or by any means, electronic or mechanical, including photocopying and recording, or by any information storage or retrieval system, except as may be expressly permitted by the 1976 Copyright Act or in writing from the publisher. Requests for permission should be addressed to Dimensions for Living, 201 Eighth Avenue South, P.O. Box 801, Nashville, TN 37202.

This book is printed on acid-free paper.

Library of Congress Cataloging-in-Publication Data

Groseclose, Kel, 1940-
  A moment with God for men: prayers for every man / Kel Groseclose.
     p.   cm.
  ISBN 0-687-08777-5 (pbk. : alk. paper)
  1. Men—Prayer-books and devotions—English.   I. Title.
BV4843.G76 1998
242'.842—dc21   98-339-57
                                                                                                CIP

Unless otherwise noted, all Scripture quotations are from the New Revised Standard Version Bible, copyright © 1989 by the Division of Christian Education of the National Council of the Churches of Christ in the United States of America, and are used by permission.

Scripture quotations noted CEV are from the Contemporary English Version of the Bible, copyright © 1995 by the American Bible Society. Scripture quotations noted JBP are from *The New Testament in Modern English*, Revised Edition, by J. B. Phillips. Copyright © J. B. Phillips, 1958, 1959, 1960, 1972. Scripture quotations noted KJV are from the King James Version of the Bible. Scripture quotations noted TLB are from *The Living Bible,* copyright © 1971 by Tyndale House Publishers, Wheaton, IL. Used by permission. Scripture quotations noted *The Message* are from *The Message: The New Testament in Contemporary English,* copyright © 1993 by Eugene H. Peterson. Published by NavPress Publishing Group.

99 00 01 02 03 04 05 06 07 — 10 9 8 7 6 5 4 3 2

MANUFACTURED IN THE UNITED STATES OF AMERICA

CONTENTS

True Greatness............ 7
Time Well Spent........... 8
Playfully Responsible 9
Put on Strength 10
Strength and Experience ... 11
Let It Go 12
A Clean Slate 13
First Love............... 14
God's Down-to-Earth Word. 15
A Joyful Servant.......... 16
Staying by the Baggage 17
A Gentle Spirit 18
Striving for Purity......... 19
The Gift of Listening 20
A Job Well Done 21

Strong Commitments. 22
Different Hats 23
When Losing Is Winning . . . 24
Fresh Every Day. 25
Motivated from Within 26
With God on the Move 27
Employees of Christ. 28
A Careful Builder. 29
Walking by Faith 30
Make It Plain 31
Am I There Yet, God? 32
Forever Chosen 33
Shouts of Joy 34
Take the Offensive 35
Get a Grip 36
True Treasure 37
Calling All Storytellers 38
Inspiration and Perspiration . 39
New Ideas 40

Wait for the Lord	41
In God's Image	42
Think About Positives	43
Perfect Timing	44
Valid Criticism	45
Hold Me Together	46
Dependent on God	47
Honest-to-God Prayers	48
An Inside Job	49
A Ministry of Presence	50
"I Love You"	51
Touched by Grace	52
Faith and Fun	53
Prune Me, Lord	54
Enjoying People	55
The Deep Places of Life	56
O God, Reveal Yourself	57
The Big Picture	58
Real Contentment	59

Emptied of Myself 60

The Riches of Wisdom 61

Maturity in Christ 62

One Day at a Time. 63

Surrounded by Saints 64

TRUE GREATNESS

"Your care for others is the measure of your greatness." —Luke 9:48c TLB

My heart, O God, knows what true greatness is, but my brain and my body keep forgetting. It's my compassion, not my credentials; my faithfulness, not my fame; my commitments, not my cars. It's inward peace, not outward power.

Remind me, Lover of My Soul, that greatness does not come from parchments hanging on walls, from balance sheets or bank accounts, from properties or political clout. From *your* eternal perspective, greatness means caring for my spouse and family, for my friends and colleagues. Teach me, day by day, that true greatness is offering a smile, giving a hug, wiping a tear, comforting a child, helping a stranger, being in love. Amen.

TIME WELL SPENT

Be careful then how you live ... making the most of the time. —*Ephesians 5:15-16*

I can fritter away time with the best of them, O Lord, but I guess you already know that. I watch sports on TV and forget to do important tasks. I play computer games or surf the Internet, and before I know it, the day's half-gone. And with the way I can worry, fret, and stew a day into oblivion, it's a wonder I ever accomplish anything!

Thank you, wise God, for expecting me to make the hours and even the minutes count, and for giving me the vision and strength to do so. I yearn to be productive, to make a difference in this world. Please whisper that message in my ear when I start frittering again. Amen.

PLAYFULLY RESPONSIBLE

Delight yourselves in the Lord, yes, find your joy in him at all times.
—*Philippians 4:4 JBP*

Creator God, you are the most dependable, reliable force in the universe. You keep this world in perfect order: Season follows season without fail; the sun rises and sets according to your precise timetable. And yet, Almighty God, you have a wonderfully playful side. You make the stars twinkle in the night sky. You cause rushing waters to sparkle and dance. You bless us with a riot of color in flowers and autumn leaves, with delicious smells and fascinating cloud shapes, with the sound of raindrops on the rooftop.

May I, like you, take delight in fulfilling my responsibilities, and may I never forget how to be playful. Amen.

PUT ON STRENGTH

Awake, awake, put on strength.
—Isaiah 51:9

I know these words from Isaiah, O Lord, anticipate your coming with power into our human lives. But they also apply to my life when I get up in the morning. I put on deodorant, clean underwear, a shirt, pants, hopefully a matching pair of socks, and my shoes. If there's time, I splash on a little cologne. The ritual continues with a cup of coffee and cold cereal or toast, and then I'm out the door, on my way.

As I go through my morning routine, remind me, God of time and eternity, to put on your Spirit's strength, to clothe myself with power from on high. (Maybe you could put a sticky note on my bathroom mirror!) Amen.

STRENGTH AND EXPERIENCE

The glory of young men is their strength; of old men, their experience.
—*Proverbs 20:29 TLB*

I remember, O God, when I was younger, stronger, and in better shape. I also thought I knew it all. Looking back now, I see how naive I was. My brain was filled with facts, but my heart and soul had so much to learn.

Years later, my body no longer has nonstop energy. I can't stay up half the night without needing a nap the next afternoon. But my inner life now is so rich and full! I still exercise and occasionally lift weights. (And my biceps aren't too bad!) Help me to realize, however, that true strength comes from emotional maturity and spiritual discernment. Amen.

LET IT GO

Do not let the sun go down on your anger.
—Ephesians 4:26b

Today, O God of compassion, I need a small favor. Could you postpone the sun's setting by an hour or so? I need extra time to calm down. I had a heated argument with someone, and I'm not feeling very forgiving. It may take a little longer than till sunset for me to stop being cranky.

I thank you, Eternal Parent, for giving us humans the gift of emotions. But sometimes mine get a bit intense. God of peace, help me never to hurt another of your precious children by being mean-spirited or abusive with my words or actions. Let me not hold grudges or carry anger in my heart for more than a few moments at a time. Amen.

A CLEAN SLATE

*If you, O LORD, should mark iniquities,
Lord, who could stand?*
—Psalm 130:3

Dear God, thank you for not keeping a permanent record of my childish mistakes, my youthful pranks and capers, my rebellious attitude, and *especially* the pain I caused my parents. I wasn't a bad kid, but I was mischievous. If you were simply judging me on all my sins over the years, I'd be down for the count. But you are the God of mercy, forgiveness, and new beginnings.

When it comes to second chances, I'm probably into the thousands by now! In all honesty, O God of everlasting patience, we both know I'm going to need a lot more. Amen.

FIRST LOVE

"I have this against you, that you have abandoned the love you had at first."
—*Revelation 2:4*

I remember when I was first in love with the young woman who later became my wife. It was an exciting, head-over-heels time. I spent most of my waking moments thinking of her. I saw only her gifts, strengths, and beauty. If she had any faults, I never noticed.

Well, I've let 12,957 days of marriage change things. Like a balloon with a slow leak, the bliss has gone down. Perhaps our love is more mature now. But I still want that spring in my step, that joy in my heart—and even that starry-eyed look I once had.

Lord, help me to show my wife that I love her now more than ever. And how much more, O God, my love for you! Amen.

GOD'S DOWN-TO-EARTH WORD

The good man eats to live, while the evil man lives to eat. —*Proverbs 13:25 TLB*

Your Word, O God, gets right to the point! You seem to know everything about me—including how I sometimes let my appetites control me. And I don't just mean those late-night raids on the refrigerator. I allow my desires for human approval, material possessions, and personal glory to shape my life.

Millennia before burgers, fries, or shakes, your Word spoke the truth. Your Spirit within me is infinitely more important than how much money I make, the car I drive, or the food I eat. Inspire me to strive for spiritual sustenance, O Lord, and let my desires be molded by my love for you. Amen.

A JOYFUL SERVANT

Let us not be weary in well-doing.
—Galatians 6:9a KJV

Let me be honest with you, O Loving Creator. At times I get bored doing the same old stuff. I become worn down from taking out the garbage every Wednesday night, watering the house plants every Saturday morning, washing the cars, mowing the lawn, walking the dog, recycling the cans and papers. The people at work expect me to be pleasant and productive every day. I'm supposed to go to church at least once a week and pay my taxes on time.

I need your inspiration, O God, to help me fulfill my duties with style and grace. May I not grump about life's repetitions, but do them joyfully. Help me to always look for the good that I can do, Lord—even in everyday situations. Amen.

STAYING BY THE BAGGAGE

"The share of the one who goes down into the battle shall be the same as the share of the one who stays by the baggage; they shall share alike." —1 Samuel 30:24b

Thank you, God, for affirming the equal value of our labors. It doesn't matter what our work is if it is honorable and if we do it for your glory. Whether we chair the board of directors or push a broom, build skyscrapers or hold a baby, handle large sums of money or sling hamburgers, we share alike in your divine approval.

Help me to do my best whether I am in the heat of battle or standing on the sidelines guarding the duffel bags. Use me wherever you need me. And may I, as you do, value people not by their job or salary but by their faithfulness and devotion. Amen.

A GENTLE SPIRIT

The fruit of the Spirit is love, joy, peace, patience, kindness, generosity, faithfulness, gentleness, and self-control.
—*Galatians 5:22-23*

My father's hands were huge and thickly callused, yet so very gentle. I can remember only being affirmed by his touch. He was calm and sweet, but a man's man—pleasantly aggressive, decisive, and strong. His life, O God, was a daily demonstration of your Spirit's fruit.

All of those nine virtues mentioned in the Scripture are intertwined with the quality of *compassion*. But none of them is for sissies or wimps. They all require spiritual discipline and inner power. Help me understand, O gentle God, that I can be a full-blooded male and yet be tender, considerate, and even sweet, if I have a pure heart and a gentle spirit. Amen.

STRIVING FOR PURITY

Keep yourself pure. —1 Timothy 5:22c

This verse from Timothy, O Lord, is certainly short and to the point. But surely you understand that we live in a world of confusing moral values. I know—you didn't give Moses the "Ten Suggestions"; you gave him commandments that you still expect us to obey. All we ask, God, is for clarity to cover the thousands of new problems and temptations we must deal with in our lives today. After all, the world has become a rather impure place where violence is glorified and sexuality is cheapened, where people wink at immorality or simply look the other way.

Give us the wisdom to know what is right and the strength to have clean thoughts, honest dealings, and pure motives. Amen.

THE GIFT OF LISTENING

To draw near to listen is better than the sacrifice offered by fools. —Ecclesiastes 5:1b

I admit it, O God: I am not a good listener. I'm often too preoccupied with my own affairs to listen to my spouse, my children, or even to you. There's so much noise in my life, I have a hard time hearing your "still small voice" (1 Kings 19:12 KJV).

Teach me the beauty of quietness. Hush me, Lord, and slow me down when I move too fast. It's amazing what I learn and how much I grow spiritually when I actually sit still and listen! Help me let go of my own agendas in order to focus on your will and your Word. Amen.

A JOB WELL DONE

And on the seventh day God finished the work that he had done, and he rested.
—Genesis 2:2

Creator God, how did you manage to rest on the seventh day? There was still much to be accomplished. You'd already done the easy stuff—created light, water, rocks, hills, and physical life for plants, animals, and people. Maybe you were resting before beginning the *really* tough job of loving and guiding your human creatures.

It seems the same for us, your servants: Our work is never finished. We complete one task only to find two more waiting in the wings. Teach us the secret of feeling good about a job well done, Lord. Help us discover the joy of accomplishing a task for its own sake—regardless of what there may be left to do. Amen.

STRONG COMMITMENTS

Commit your way to the LORD.
—*Psalm 37:5a*

I say yes when I mean no. I make commitments but then, at the last minute, back out; or I quit part of the way through because I didn't count the cost in terms of time and energy. Sometimes I try to do too much and spread myself too thin.

Faithful, covenantal God, you who make eternal commitments, help this poor human man. May I build lasting friendships; a strong marriage; and abiding ties to family, church, and community. Place in my heart the longing and the will to make permanent and deep commitments—beginning, O God, with you. Amen.

DIFFERENT HATS

I have become all things to all people.
—1 Corinthians 9:22b

Saint Paul actually *achieved* this goal; *I'm* still *working* on it. I have a lot of hats. The ones on the closet shelf, I seldom wear. But the *other* hats—those of son, brother, husband, father, grandparent, friend, colleague, employee—I wear all the time. In some of those hats, I'm comfortable, maybe even dashing. In others I look comical. When I'm the boss one moment and a household servant the next, I get my hats mixed up. *Someday* I'll be able to keep them straight.

In the meantime, Lord, please help me be true to myself while I'm changing hats, putting one back on the shelf and another on my head. Amen.

WHEN LOSING IS WINNING

"Those who try to make their life secure will lose it, but those who lose their life will keep it." —Luke 17:33

O God, I don't like losing. I'm a competitive person. I enjoy winning at sports—golf, table tennis, even playing "horse" on the hoop over the garage door.

Be patient with me, Lord, while I learn the spiritual truth that losing is winning. Let me lose—my pride, to become truly humble; my energy, in the act of serving others; my self-centeredness, to accept your will. It doesn't matter whether I win on the tennis court, on the softball field, or even playing Trivial Pursuit. But by giving my life to you, O God, I gain eternity. Now *that's winning!*

FRESH EVERY DAY

[God's] mercies never come to an end; they are new every morning.
—Lamentations 3:22b-23a

O God, I'm thankful your mercies are fresh every morning, because my soul and body just *aren't*. I am *not* a morning person. Your love is indeed unconditional if you love me when I first roll out of bed—bad breath, creases on my face, hair sticking out, and eyes stuck shut. Like manna in the wilderness, your grace is fresh every day. There's no expiration date stamped on our relationship.

But it's morning again, Lord, and I'm trying to prepare for the tasks that lie ahead. A cup of coffee will help. But give me an extra measure of your fresh, new mercies, or I'll never make it. Amen.

MOTIVATED FROM WITHIN

Do not lag in zeal, be ardent in spirit, serve the Lord. —Romans 12:11

O Lord, my motivational dipstick shows I'm a couple of quarts low right now. I don't seem to have much enthusiasm. I've been doing what's required, but there's not much joy when life seems to be nothing more than duty. I feel that I need to "get going," but I know that I cannot do this all by myself.

Lord, give me some vitamin Z (for zeal) to perk up my spirit; help me find motivation inside my own heart; light a spiritual fire under me. Rekindle my devotion to you, O God, and restore to me the delight of being your disciple. Amen.

WITH GOD ON THE MOVE

*The LORD will keep
your going out and your coming in
from this time on and forevermore.
—Psalm 121:8*

Lord, thank you for this promise! You are with me on my daily commute when horns honk and tires squeal. You're there—and not just in the quiet pew on Sunday morning or when I pause to pray; your Spirit is with me at the busy gas station, the business lunch in a crowded restaurant, the long line at the bank, and my child's noisy ball game. You've been around since the beginning of history, yet you're quite capable of keeping up with today's hectic pace.

In all my comings and goings, Lord, be my constant companion—now and for always. Amen.

EMPLOYEES OF CHRIST

Work hard and cheerfully at all you do, just as though you were working for the Lord . . . remembering that it is the Lord Christ who is going to pay you. . . . He is the one you are really working for.
—*Colossians 3:23-24 TLB*

Someone else may pay my salary, but I actually work for you, O Lord. I'm part of your staff; I'm on your eternal payroll. That means your Word contains my job description. I'm glad you're the Boss. I like your style of leadership—firm, gentle, and fair. Of course, there's no time clock; you expect twenty-four hours of honest labor every day. It's *definitely* a full-time job! But as the old joke goes, your retirement plan is out of this world. Help me to work hard for you. Amen.

A CAREFUL BUILDER

Let every man take heed how he buildeth.
—1 Corinthians 3:10b KJV

I'm a klutz when it comes to mechanical things. I'm sure you've watched me, O Lord, struggling to install a new faucet, fix a leaky toilet, or hang a closet door. I eventually complete the task, but not until I've made ten trips to the hardware store. Likewise, sometimes I'm not too graceful when it comes to building my inner life.

You laid the foundation in Jesus Christ. Guide me that I may build with care, integrity, and love. O Master Builder, please give this klutz help in constructing strong, enduring relationships with you and with others. Amen.

WALKING BY FAITH

For we walk by faith, not by sight.
—2 Corinthians 5:7

Walking home yesterday I did something I hadn't done since childhood. As I came through the park, I shut my eyes and walked as far as I dared. I made it to fifty paces. My steps grew shorter and shorter, and I was headed right for a tree. But it was exciting: I made it!

God, be patient with me as I learn to walk not by sight, but by faith in you. Hold my hand when I get scared. Nudge me in the other direction when I'm heading for danger. Lead me down the paths you would have me travel, Lord, and may I totally trust you every step of the way. Amen.

MAKE IT PLAIN

Tell me what to do, O Lord, and make it plain. —Psalm 27:11 TLB

Sometimes I'm a bit dense, O God. It takes me a while to figure out what you want for my life. In the midst of daily stresses and struggles, I need you to be direct. Tell me the truth, Lord, and make it plain. If I still don't get it, be blunt.

I thank you for the clarity and simplicity of your Word. Yes, there are names I can't pronounce and directions I have trouble following. But you couldn't be more to the point than when you promise to love me forever. Thank you for your persistent yet gentle honesty. Amen.

AM I THERE YET, GOD?

I have not yet reached my goal, and I am not perfect.... I don't feel that I have already arrived.
—*Philippians 3:12-13 CEV*

"Am I there yet, God? Have I fulfilled your hopes and completed your work? Have I reached spiritual perfection?"

"No, my son, you haven't. You never will in this life. So relax and enjoy the trip. I created you to learn and grow, to share and serve in every moment from birth to death."

"But I need to see results and have closure in my life."

"I know, and soon enough you will. In the meantime, notice the beauty around you, hold hands with others on the journey, and welcome each new day with joy."

"With your help, O Lord, I'll give it my best." Amen.

FOREVER CHOSEN

He chose us in Christ before the foundation of the world.   —Ephesians 1:4

I always wanted to be the first kid chosen when we played baseball at the park. I certainly didn't want to be the *last* one picked! In truth, I was usually chosen somewhere in the middle. But you, O Lord, selected me in Christ even before you created this earth. Do you know how that makes me feel? *Of course* you do! It gives me confidence; it makes me feel needed. I'm an important part of your team, God, and not just a last-minute addition. You have chosen me for eternity. What a blessed thought! Amen.

SHOUTS OF JOY

"He will yet fill your mouth with laughter, and your lips with shouts of joy."
—*Job 8:21*

God, I know that life has its inevitable low spots. I can't always go around dancing on my toes and whistling a happy tune. But when the demands become great and the pressures intense, remind me of the promise you made to a sorrowing, long-suffering Job: to fill him with laughter.

I get cranky when a driver doesn't go immediately after the light changes to green. I grumble when things at work sometimes don't go my way. O Lord, help me to realize that such things are only temporary. Remove from me all grouchiness, and replace my mutterings with shouts of joy! Amen.

TAKE THE OFFENSIVE

Don't allow yourself to be overpowered by evil. Take the offensive—overpower evil with good! —Romans 12:21 JBP

I never was much of a football player, but I *did* learn that it's easier to play defense than offense. On defense, you mostly just try to flatten your opponent and tackle whoever's got the ball. On offense, you have to learn plays, know blocking assignments, and run precise pass routes.

O Divine Coach, give me a pep talk so that I won't simply sit on the bench while life in this world passes me by. Teach me to take the offensive, to look for opportunities, and to have a game plan based on your goodness, beauty, love, and truth. Amen.

GET A GRIP

So take a new grip with your tired hands, stand firm on your shaky legs.
—Hebrews 12:12 TLB

I've always been proud, Lord, of my firm handshake. But some days, by the time evening rolls around, I feel puny. My back is sore, my head hurts, and my whole body aches with pain. The demands and frustrations have built up. That's when I like to relax at home—watch the news, read the paper, hold a purring cat on my lap, have a rocking-chair snuggle with a granddaughter. Thank you, God, for providing so many ways to restore my energy, for helping me get a new grip on life. Amen.

TRUE TREASURE

"For where your treasure is, there your heart will be also." —*Matthew 6:21*

Give me wisdom, O God, to know what is truly valuable. Give me discernment to know those things that have eternal significance; then give me the courage to make them the focus of my life. I am so easily deceived by anything that glitters—by riches, fame, and popularity, by big salaries, fancy cars, and political clout.

Gracious God, teach me to treasure my soul, my inner life; to prize people and relationships above mere things; to cherish your Spirit's presence. Fill my heart with the treasures of hope and love and joy. Amen.

CALLING ALL STORYTELLERS

How are they to believe in one of whom they have never heard? And how are they to hear without someone to proclaim him?
—*Romans 10:14*b, c

Lord, I know exactly who that someone is. It's regular folks like me who sometimes get shaky knees, who stammer a lot and may be shy and self-conscious when speaking before an audience. But then, you really don't care about eloquence, do you? It's honesty and caring that you want. A glib tongue can't begin to compare with a warm heart. We're not talking about full-scale sermons, but about simple, deep confessions of personal faith.

Inspire me, God, to tell the old, old story of Jesus and his love in compelling and creative ways. Amen.

INSPIRATION AND PERSPIRATION

We know that all things work together for good for those who love God.
—*Romans 8:28*

I frequently recall this verse when something bad happens. Dear God, I assume all you have to do is snap your all-powerful fingers and everything will be fine. But there's one little word in this sentence I conveniently forget: "all things *work* together." You expect me to do my part, don't you, Lord? We are partners, and we're supposed to work together. My job is to labor for you: to pray, study, worship, witness, and serve your people everywhere. Our relationship is to be a wonderful blend of divine inspiration and human perspiration.

Help me to be your good and faithful partner, Lord, in your work. Amen.

NEW IDEAS

The intelligent man is always open to new ideas. In fact, he looks for them.
—*Proverbs 18:15 TLB*

One of the things I like about you, God, is how you're always coming up with new ideas. Every sunrise (and sunset) is different, every flower is unique, every human being is a one-of-a-kind individual. New life abounds on this planet!

Your Word instructs us to sing to you new songs. Keep me open to new attitudes, ideas, and people. Don't ever let me say, "But we've always done it *this* way." Shake me, unsettle me when I get in a rut, that I may forever be receptive to your eternally fresh and creative ways. Amen.

WAIT FOR THE LORD

Wait for the LORD;
be strong, and let your heart take
courage.
—Psalm 27:14

I've always had a hard time waiting—even waiting for dinner to be ready or standing in line for tickets to a new movie. Too often I put the proverbial cart before the horse: I've gotten more than my share of lumps from trying to go through doors before they were opened.

It helps, O God, that you understand. You know how difficult it is for us humans to wait. That's why the psalmist tells us to be strong and have courage. Unless I wait for you, Lord, there are experiences I will never have, truths I will never learn, and a love whose depths I will never know. Amen.

IN GOD'S IMAGE

*So God created humankind in his image,
in the image of God he created them;
male and female he created them.*
—*Genesis 1:27*

Looking back, God, do you ever ponder why you first created man and then woman? Much of the time, it seems that it should have been the other way around. Through the centuries, we males have acted as though we're in charge of the world; and we've made a mess of it. Too often we've behaved aggressively, arrogantly, and abusively.

O God, please send us a male liberation movement to free our attitudes, release our emotions, and nurture our spiritual lives. Encourage us as men to truly reflect your image and to treat our fellow human beings with the same loving care in which you created us all. Amen.

THINK ABOUT POSITIVES

If there is any excellence and if there is anything worthy of praise, think about these things. —*Philippians 4:8*b

Does it distress you, God, the way our world focuses on negative things? Human failings, tragedies, and global disasters dominate the headlines. Yes, they're all very real and very painful. But they aren't the whole story.

There's so much good in your world— so much beauty and creativity and so many loving deeds. Help us, Lord, to deal honestly with our problems and to face them squarely. But remind us also to emphasize positive qualities and to look for things worthy of praise. Amen.

PERFECT TIMING

For everything there is a season, and a time for every matter under heaven.
—Ecclesiastes 3:1

Day and night, the tide's ebb and flow, earth's seasons, the planets in their orbits—all these you have set in flawless order, O God. Your sense of timing is incomparable. Best of all was your knowing the exact moment in history for the Incarnation, precisely when to send Jesus to us.

You also set a rhythm to our earthly lives. You offer us wisdom to know when to plant and when to harvest, when to speak and when to keep silent, when to work and when to rest. From birth to death to eternity, your Spirit leads us. Praise be to you, O God of perfect timing!

VALID CRITICISM

It is a badge of honor to accept valid criticism. —Proverbs 25:12 TLB

I usually get my feelings hurt at first when someone criticizes me, even when that criticism is constructive. I guess that just proves I'm human. But then, O God, your Spirit enters the situation. I take a step back and reflect on the person's comment. If the words are true, I'm able to take them to heart. And it helps when the criticism is offered kindly and with compassion.

Most important of all, God, is that I be receptive to *your* helpful suggestions and open to *your* loving criticisms. Give me a mind big enough to accept honest judgments—not grudgingly, but as badges of honor. Amen.

HOLD ME TOGETHER

[Christ] himself is before all things, and in him all things hold together.
—*Colossians 1:17*

The world around me seems to go faster and faster with every passing year. It becomes increasingly difficult for me to hang on. Things change so quickly that my head spins. I could ask you, God, to put on the brakes, but I know that's not in your plan. Instead, I'll claim for myself the "holding together" power of your son, Jesus. When I'm feeling pushed and pulled this way and that, infuse me with energy to keep going and with wisdom to know those things that truly matter. When I do fall, catch me in your loving arms, dust me off, and set me again to working for you. Amen.

DEPENDENT ON GOD

"My grace is sufficient for you, for power is made perfect in weakness."
—*2 Corinthians 12:9*a

If you, God, had to file a tax return, we'd all be listed as your dependents, wouldn't we? You don't just supply *half* of our support; you're *it*—the sum total. Everything we have comes from you.

But I have this basic problem: I like to think I'm on my own; I can take care of myself; I'm really quite a strong person. Okay, I'm stubborn; I know that's not an attitude conducive to spiritual growth. I'm working on it.

Please be patient, Lord, as I learn that to be independent I must be *your* dependent, that your strength is available to me in my weakness. Amen.

HONEST-TO-GOD PRAYERS

"When you are praying, do not heap up empty phrases." —*Matthew 6:7*

I'm guessing, Dear God, that you like children's prayers for the same reasons I do: They're refreshingly blunt, have a touch of humor, and are usually short. Then we children grow up and think we're supposed to pray to you using lots of words—and big ones, too.

It should be quite obvious you aren't impressed with human eloquence or grammatical correctness. If I understand the words of your son correctly, you appreciate honesty, directness, and integrity. You value one word from our hearts more than a thousand off the top of our heads. What's the point of rambling on anyway? You know our thoughts even before we say a thing!

AN INSIDE JOB

Don't let the world around you squeeze you into its own mould, but let God re-make you so that your whole attitude of mind is changed. —Romans 12:2 JBP

The world certainly knows how to put the squeeze on us, O God. We're told that moral values are outdated; that it doesn't matter what we believe; that giving you one hour of our time every Sunday morning is more than enough. We're bombarded by claims for products, ideologies, and institutions. The constant pressure makes our heads hurt.

Our salvation is that you have remolded our minds from within. You have given wisdom to discern the truth and strength to resist all lesser claims. It still isn't easy, Lord. So stay close by when the squeeze is on. Amen.

A MINISTRY OF PRESENCE

I hope to spend some time with you, if the Lord permits. —1 Corinthians 16:7b

The apostle Paul understood that while he might write wonderful letters, there was no substitute for being with the people of his churches. This is true for us as well. We need to rub elbows with others of your followers—to worship and work together, to pray and play together. You call us to spend time together, to stand beside one another, to support one another on our faith journeys.

O God of the Incarnation, help us be there for our families, our business colleagues, a lonely neighbor, a hurting friend. Equip us for a ministry of your loving Presence. Amen.

"I LOVE YOU"

"You shall love the Lord your God with all your heart, and with all your soul, and with all your mind, and with all your strength." —Mark 12:30

Lord, I love you. I love your son Jesus. There, I said it! I don't get around to saying that very often, do I? I could claim it's because I'm busy or that I'm the strong, silent type. I'm a man who lets my actions speak for me. The truth is, I really don't know how to verbalize love.

You aren't the only one, Lord, who seldom hears these words from me; I don't often say them to my family, either. Do I somehow feel that saying those three words might make me appear weak or less masculine?

Open my heart and loosen my tongue, O God, that I may speak of love. Amen.

TOUCHED BY GRACE

With [Saul] went warriors whose hearts God had touched. —1 Samuel 10:26b

I'm not much of a warrior—at least not in terms of ages past. Yet I still pray, O God, that you will touch my heart. When I'm at work, touch my heart that I may fulfill my job with faithfulness. When I'm at home, touch my heart that I may unconditionally love my family. When I'm snuggled into my bed at night, touch my heart with peace. And when I must make difficult decisions and say painfully honest words, when I am called upon to be strong and bold—a modern-day warrior—*especially* then, make me sensitive and tender. Touch my heart with grace. Amen.

FAITH AND FUN

Jesus said to them, "The wedding guests cannot mourn as long as the bridegroom is with them, can they?" —Matthew 9:15

I'm guessing that your son Jesus and his disciples were a fun-loving group. They worked hard and were intent on sharing their faith. But they also laughed a lot. Jesus told stories, went to wedding parties, invited people to feasts, enjoyed fishing trips with the Twelve. Stodgy Pharisees accused them of having too much fun. Well, some of your disciples today are more like those Pharisees—tense and glum.

O God, remind us that we serve a Risen Savior. Put smiles on our faces, a spring in our steps, and songs of joy in our hearts! Amen.

PRUNE ME, LORD

"Every branch that bears fruit he prunes to make it bear more fruit." —John 15:2b

God of grace, you know how much I love the dwarf apricot tree in our backyard. You also know how hard it is for me to trim parts of it off. But it must be pruned if it is to continue bearing fruit. That's because while old wood provides strength and stability, it's the *new* growth where fruit buds and delicious apricots appear.

Lord, it's even more difficult for me to let you prune my life. I resist change. I don't want to let go of old patterns, attitudes, and ideas. Yet I want to grow spiritually and be a productive follower, a fruitful branch on the vine of your kingdom. So prune me, dear Lord, as it pleases you, and help me to be more than I am now. Amen.

ENJOYING PEOPLE

The Holy Spirit, God's gift, does not want you to be afraid of people, but to be wise and strong, and to love them and enjoy being with them. —2 Timothy 1:7 TLB

After a long day at the office, Lord, I sometimes resemble a porcupine with its quills sticking out. "Leave me alone," I communicate, "or you'll wish you had!" I love people, but I grow weary from the demands of family, work, and community service.

Jesus enjoyed people too, yet he regularly went off by himself to meditate. Maybe my problem is that I'm escaping rather than seeking spiritual refreshment. Even when I need time alone, God, grant me a sweet, loving spirit. Remind me to keep my quills and sharp edges tucked in. Amen.

THE DEEP PLACES OF LIFE

Out of the depths I cry to you, O LORD. Lord, hear my voice!
—*Psalm 130:1-2a*

Be with me, God, in the deep places of life. When I am struggling to make major decisions, give me wisdom. When I am in the depths of sorrow, comfort me. When my relationships are troubled or broken, bolster my strength. Bestow upon me an extra measure of your grace. And Lord, when my joy knows no bounds; when my faith is rock solid; when I am totally immersed in love; hear then my prayers of gratitude; receive my heart's delight. Go with me into life's profound experiences, O God, and I shall be safe. Amen.

O GOD, REVEAL YOURSELF

O that you would tear open the heavens and come down. —Isaiah 64:1a

Lord, you did exactly what the prophet Isaiah asked when you sent Jesus to earth. Your loving Word became flesh and dwelt among us. Yet still we've managed to make a mess of things. We've fought wars more than we've made peace, ignored injustice and immorality, allowed violence to go unchecked, grown callous to poverty, forgotten the homeless, and in general have gone our merry way.

I'm not asking you to clean up after us or to fix everything we've broken. But please, dear God, send an outpouring of your Holy Spirit to stir our hearts, to rekindle our imaginations, to make your true self known, and to revive us again! Amen.

THE BIG PICTURE

*The earth is the LORD's and all that is in it,
the world, and those who live in it.*
—Psalm 24:1

It's all yours, God, the whole kit and caboodle. Therefore, give me a world view; help me see the big picture, in which I'm just a small part. I want to show concern for creation and for everyone on the face of this planet. I can't know each person by name. I can't solve every global problem; I'm human. But I *can* be informed and aware. I can be compassionate and loving and take care of my small corner. Don't let my love be limited by personal concerns or my mind be trapped by my own small understandings. Holy Spirit, give me an ever-growing vision of your plan. Amen.

REAL CONTENTMENT

Keep your lives free from the love of money, and be content with what you have.
—*Hebrews 13:5*a

I confess, God, that I have a tough time measuring up to this text. I own a great deal. Our house is filled with possessions. There's money in the bank—not a lot, but enough. The refrigerator and cupboards aren't bare, that's for sure. Even the garage is crammed with "stuff." Yet I always seem to want more—a bigger income, a fancier house, a racier car.

Speak to me with bluntness, O God of wisdom. Remind me that loving relationships are more important than outward possessions. Let me not be rich in things and poor in soul. Give me the blessing of contentment, and let me give thanks for what I have. Amen.

EMPTIED OF MYSELF

Let the same mind be in you that was in Christ Jesus,
   who, though he was in the form of God,
   did not regard equality with God
   as something to be exploited,
  but emptied himself.
              —*Philippians 2:5-7*a

O God, there are times when I become so full of myself there's no room for others or even for you. Help me pour out my self-centeredness to make more space for your love. After all, I pull the plug to let dirty water drain from the bathtub before I refill it with fresh water.

Encourage me to empty out my small problems in order to respond to the needs of those around me. Let me pour out my life and be filled with your Spirit. Amen.

THE RICHES OF WISDOM

To be wise is as good as being rich; in fact, it is better. —*Ecclesiastes 7:11 TLB*

Riches rise and fall with interest rates and stock market prices. But wisdom abides; and unlike riches, O God, it is available to all who turn to you and earnestly desire it. You offer good judgment and understanding to those who study your Word. Knowledge and clear thinking come to those who seek your will.

Gaining wisdom is a lifetime journey. Let me be more committed to growing intellectually than to accumulating wealth. Whether I am in poverty or affluence or somewhere in between, may I pursue wisdom and its eternal blessings. Amen.

MATURITY IN CHRIST

Let's leave the preschool fingerpainting exercises on Christ and get on with the grand work of art. Grow up in Christ.
—*Hebrews 6:1*, The Message

Sometimes, O God, I behave like the immature little boy I used to be. I want my way, have to be told what to do, and avoid responsibilities. It's as though I say to you, "If I'm not up to the plate first, I'll take my bat and ball and go home."

Help me to grow up in Christ—to follow him wherever he leads me, to become his true disciple and a more effective servant. I want a childlike soul, open, trusting, and pure. But when it comes to spiritual maturity, I aspire to full manhood. Amen.

ONE DAY AT A TIME

"So don't be anxious about tomorrow. God will take care of your tomorrow too. Live one day at a time." —Matthew 6:34 TLB

O God, help me be alive right now! I'm someone who likes to "borrow trouble," who worries about problems before they occur. Lord, there's no shortage of lenders willing to let your children borrow anxiety, but the terms are tough and the interest rates sky-high.

Teach me to make solid plans for my future yet enjoy each day to the full. May I not postpone living while worrying about possible problems or anticipating coming joys. Yesterday is part of history, and tomorrow hasn't arrived. Help me squeeze every bit of life out of this present moment. Amen.

SURROUNDED BY SAINTS

Therefore, since we are surrounded by so great a cloud of witnesses, let us also lay aside every weight and the sin that clings so closely, and let us run with perseverance the race that is set before us.   —Hebrews 12:1

Remind me, O God, that I'm not alone. Your Spirit is my constant companion, and I'm surrounded by saints who've come before. I'm part of a magnificent faith community! I'm blessed with both friends on earth and friends above; I'm connected to eternity by tender ties of love. What power! What joy! I can actually feel the support of that great cloud of witnesses. I'm ready, Lord, to run the race and to persevere when the way is steep. Amen.